Fairytales & Lies

Jennifer Derby

Fairytales & Lies

Jennifer Derby

Illustrations and cover design © 2021 by Fay Helfer
fayhelfer.com • fay@fayhelfer.com • @fayhelfer

ISBN-13: 978-0-578-95786-9

Fairytales & Lies

Jennifer Derby

If you think
this book
is about you,
you're right.

Contents

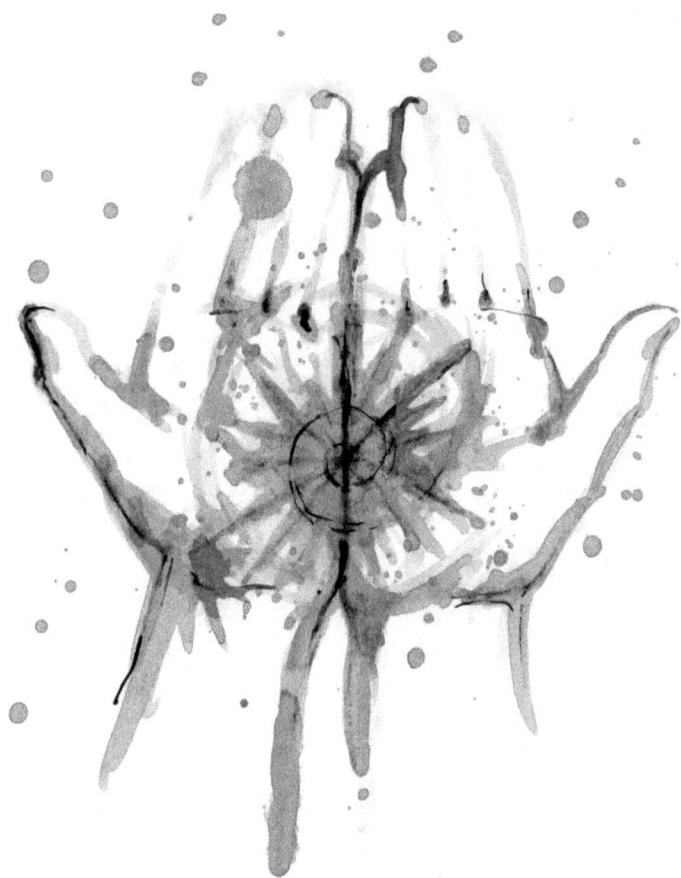

Little did you know
All those years ago
That you held in your hands
The very first preview.

Thank you for your unending support
Thank you for loving me
Thank you for the journey
Thank you for it all.

Prologue

We Fell Like Summer

It was the weather, I think, that made falling in love so effortless. Light, and cool, and breezy. Sunbeams that kissed your skin just-warm-enough on an otherwise cool day. The kind of early-summer bliss that makes you giddy and carefree.

Radiant like new hibiscus flowers unfurling in the sunshine.
Comfortable and easy like a hammock swaying in the shade of the sea-grape trees.
Refreshing, yet intoxicating like the rum and coconut water in your glass.
Soothing like the sound of the waves lapping up on shore; the ocean whispering sweetly to her muse.

Your love descended upon me in much the same way; light and refreshing; warm and easy; soothing and comfortable. Your soul whispered to mine and I was immediately intoxicated with the everything that was you.

I lived and breathed you.
I lived and breathed you.
I lived and breathed you.

I loved and grieved you...

Fairytales Not Included

"If it all spilled out, I would be so ashamed."

"But then, why do you write it? Solidify it, for the world to see?"

"Because we all have stories, really. And none of them look like fairytales."

ACT I: The Loving

Come And Be Still

Come and let your fingertips whisper softly to my skin
And your breath fall easy on my shoulders
Come and tell me tales with your kiss alone
While the rush of my goosebumps listens closer

Come and let your mind undress me in the dark
Let your eyes caress my every curve
Come and speak the language only my body understands
While my tongue hangs delicately on every word

Come and let your eyelashes brush my collarbone
And your love drip unhurried down my neck
Come and let your scent caress my body
While your taste rests sweetly on my lips

Come and let the cool air between us be warmed
And your body become one with mine
Come and let the beads dance gracefully lower
While my skin cries silently from lost time

Come and let your soul inhale me fully
Let your lungs pilfer my every breath
Come and stir a fervent desire in my belly
While logic and time fall to their deaths

Come and let our hearts converse as one
And let us be still together
Come and collapse all my walls with your bliss
While we thirst for this moment to last forever

You

You.
That's it.
That's all.
Just, you.

You occupy so much of me.
My thoughts.
My dreams.
Minutes, hours, and days.

Ever-present, and yet so far away.
Always here and yet never by my side.

How'd you get so close?
How'd I let you in?
You.

You Got In

I don't know how you did it.
How you squeezed your way in.
How you got
Over
Under
Around those walls.
Made me feel again.
Feel everything.
The good
The bad
The everything.
Sparked fire in my soul.
Sparked a new—
A renewed life.
Snuck in.
Just snuck quietly
Past all guards.
Somehow you snuck in.
Somehow,
I let you.
Let you in.

My heart was closed.
And somehow
You
Cracked its thick skin.

I Know You

You think
I don't know you.
The dark parts.
The parts that are hidden.
The parts you won't let surface.
The parts that few see.
When you're unabashedly
Unrestricted
And unrestrained.
The parts you think
You should be
Ashamed
Of.

The truth is
I know you.
I know it all
Already.
And the surprising thing is
That there isn't
Too much there
That would surprise me.

You think it impossible.
But I know it all
And love you
With a love
Unlike any
You've ever known
Anyway.

Unfold

I can't wait to feel your hands on me. One on the small of my back, the other on the back of my neck as you pull me in. Closer. I can taste your lips. I breathe deep. I've missed you. You relinquish my lips as I exhale and you move down my neck. You find that spot. That one. Just in the crook. A hard place to find, but one that's also hard to keep secret once you've hit it. My body reacts and gives it away. I drop my head back, exhale again, and pull you in closer. You kiss, suck, bite. You know how to make me Lose. My. Mind.

Stormy Sunday Afternoon

I want you.
A rainy, stormy
Sunday afternoon.
A glass of champagne.
And nothing else to do.

No commitments.
No obligations.
No time constraints.
No lists. No goals.
Nobody waiting.

Just us
And the covers
And the rain outside.

Darlin'

I love it when he calls me darlin',
Softly grasps the back of my neck,
Kisses me sweet and long and hard,
And treats me with respect.

Bad Habits

You are my best mistake
And my worst vice.

.

When otherwise strong
You are my weakness.

I exercise restraint
But with you, my boundaries are meaningless.

I'm straight-laced and tightly bound
But you unravel me.

I maintain self-control
But get lost in your sea.

.

You distract and arouse me
With your stillness alone.

.

With a single touch
Heat rises to my skin.

While a kiss well placed
Simultaneously gives me chills.

How you make me shiver
When I'm hot deep inside.

The sound of your breath
Sends me into overdrive.

.

Melt me

.

Let me breathe you in
So addicted to your high.

Let me drink of your whiskey
And get drunk off your rye.

Let me shoot you up
And feel you course through my veins.

My head's in a fog
But it's clear I need you again.

.

Your eyes, your smell, your touch, your love
Linger on my body like smoke and rain.

Giving rise to sensations
Hours after you came.

Your taste leaves me yearning
For my next passionate hit.

Itching to get back to you
For my next fucking fix.

.

It's impossible not to indulge
I'm addicted, it's true.

I'm so high off your lovin'
I love the drug that is you.

Disturbing the Peace

...it's ironic, she said,
I'm so quiet when I masturbate...

~ How to wake the neighbors.

Calming Chaos

You love me, I think, not because I need you—but because I don't. Because I'll let you take care of me even though you know this is hard. Somewhere, underneath the veil of thick skin and nonchalance, you know me better than anyone. You see my strength and aren't intimidated by it, yet you know somewhere along the line there's going to come a time when I'll fall apart, maybe in silence, in darkness, and very discreetly, but fall apart nonetheless. And you know that besides being the only one who knows and understands this, you're just the strength I'll need to get back up again.

And you find a purpose in loving me. A reason to care openly for someone in a way you have never allowed yourself to before. A way to be vulnerable and, even though it's scary, a way to let me in, too, for the first time in—in ever. Because you know that I'll never judge, I'll accept your wounds and your scars, and I'll love you through them all.

And we'll grow together in this way. Giving strength and getting stronger. And through the giving, and with time, allowing ourselves to break down walls, be vulnerable, and most of all trusting. Because more than anything this for us is the hardest part - to trust and know that love will be there to catch us - when it had only eluded, abandoned, judged, and misunderstood us before. And our hearts find a calm and peace, where once only chaos existed.

~ Nighttime Musings

Your hands
On the back of my neck
Whilst you kiss me soft and slow.

That moment.

The Smell of Your Shirt

I want to get lost in you.

Hold me.

Hold me so that all I smell is you.
So that when I press my head against your chest I breathe you in and all I can taste is you;
So that when I pull you close and you close me in your arms, there in that momentary retreat, everything else fades away.

And when I breathe you in, my head clears and my mind shifts there is only you and me.
So that nothing in the world matters but the smell of your shirt and the touch of your skin against mine.

Hold me.
And I'm lost. In you.

That Too

My heart still tugs me straight to you.

And your thumb on my cheek and fingers on the back of my neck;
And the way you pull me close to kiss me, sweet but strong...

That too.

Intertwined

...Arms...
...Legs...
...Sheets...
...Skin...
...Lips...
...Breath...

...Hard to tell where you end and I begin;
And I love you intertwined with me...

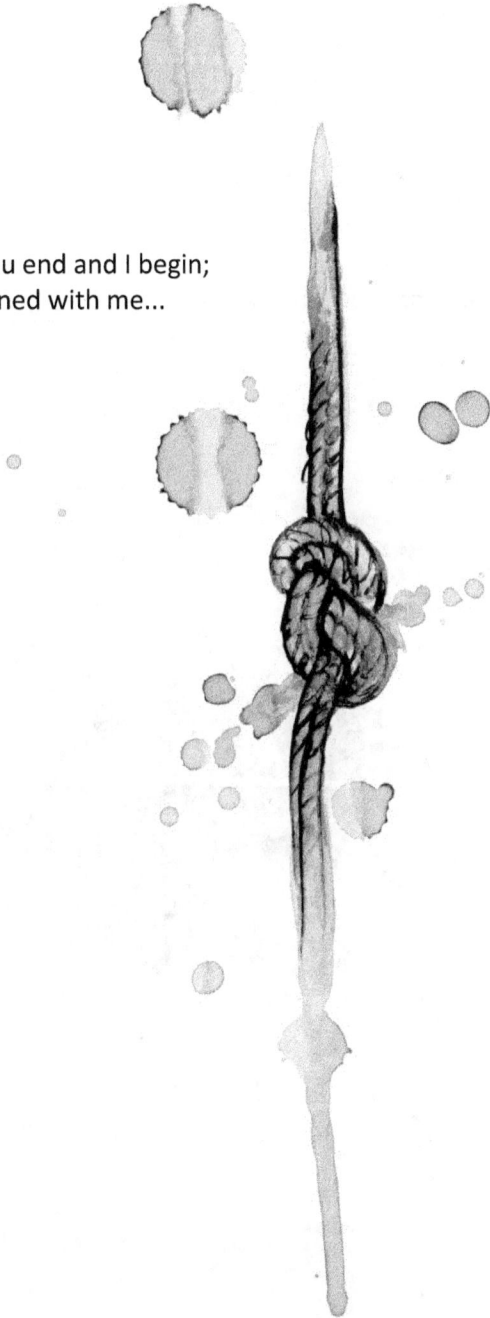

Sound

That sound.
You sneak it out of me every time.
I'm so happy—in heaven—that
I'm angry at the giddiness
That easily and freely lets you know
The state I'm in.

I exhale
And I make that goddamn sound.

Summer Storm

You are my thunder.
The strong, steady,
Unwavering roar.
With a faithful, rolling rumble
You call out to me.

I am your rain.
Singing sweetly,
I fall softly into you.
As my delicate drops pour down
In sync to your beckoning,
Tiny droplets bead
And roll gently off your skin,
Covering all of you
In all of me.

Our connection
Is magnetic;
The way you call to me,
And I fall for you,
In this rhythm,
Dance,
Song,
We call love.

Longing for a space and time
We can be more
Than a fleeting summer storm.

You are my rolling thunder
My love is your rain
We are the storm
Inseparable.

Damn You

Damn you.

What have you done to me?

There's not one hour
Of one single day
That I don't
Think about you.

Every moment
I'm consumed with you.
Like a silly,
Love-struck teenager.
In everything I do,
I wonder,
what would you
Do,
Think,
Say?

Would you comfort me in times of trouble?
Make me feel safe
With the knack you have for
Always making me feel better?
Would we just sit and watch tv?
Binge-watch some Netflix series?
Nap quietly on the couch on a rainy, lazy,
Sunday afternoon?
Could you even sit still that long...?

Would I—could I—feel
Your hand slide gently up my leg?
Maybe a soft kiss here and there.
Maybe we'd just laugh awhile
About stupid, ridiculous
Inside jokes.

You would rub my feet
And I'd kiss you softly.
I'd make you feel at home.
Just my fingertips on your skin.
Just even only being able to
Touch and kiss you
Whenever I wanted to.

Whenever you wanted me to.

Would these fake conversations
And nonsensical musings in my mind
Ever actually come to pass?

Would I be able to lay my head
Gently on your chest
And listen while you breathe?
Fall asleep to the sound of
Your heart beating in sync with mine?

Every moment, it's you.
Every minute
You're there.
You live in the layers
Between my every other thought.

I hate it
And love it
All at the same time.
I think myself a fool
For loving you.

God damn you.

What have you done to me?

Paradox

You are my source of anger—
And tremendous happiness.

My constant chaos—
And my deepest calm.

The place I feel safest—
And yet most vulnerable.

The one I've just discovered—
And who I've known forever.

My greatest despair—
And my deepest peace.

My harshest critic—
And my biggest fan.

My source of unsteadiness—
And the rock I stand firm on.

The one who gives me space to breathe—
And who takes my breath away.

My greatest heartache—
And the one who's touched my soul.

(The one I cannot be with—
And yet cannot be without.)

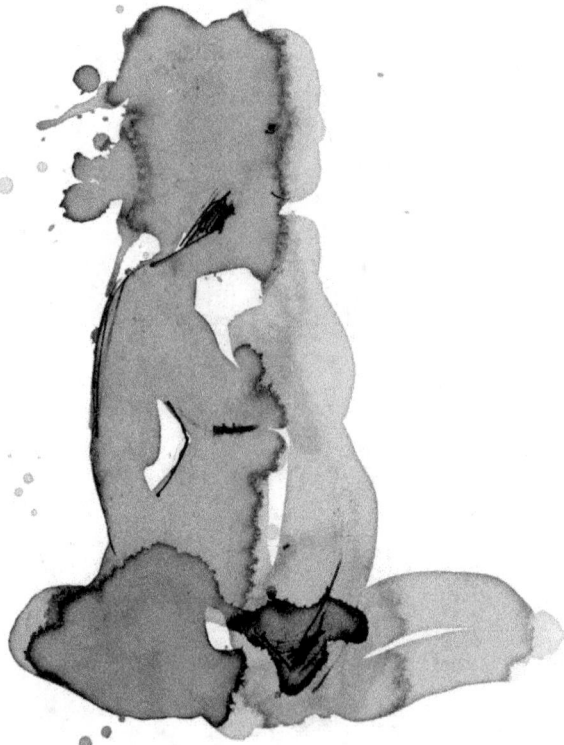

ACT II: The Missing

I Wish I Wrote More

I wish I wrote more. More about you. About the crazy, unexpected way you make me feel. Even when I try to convince myself otherwise. When I try telling myself that it's better another way. A different way. You capture me, a simple gaze and half a smile make me doubt all other realities and let me know what I feel for you is real.

I wish I wrote more about the way it makes me feel to flip you the bird, call you some dirty name, throw you an f-bomb and have you laugh at me. How your sick sense of humor, that so closely matches mine, makes me feel like home. No one has ever made me laugh like you. How my not having to worry about expressing myself with you frees me and allows me to let my guard down just that much more. I don't have to censor, for the first time in my life, and I can actually be me.

I wish I wrote more about how you make me feel when I can bitch and moan and lament about stupid work shit and you'll commiserate with me. About how at the end of the day, after all the commiserating is done, you teach me, convince me, remind me, of what's really important. And the long, tiring day melts away. How your keeping me engaged in some long, philosophical discussion about odd, provocative, completely meaningless or tremendously insightful topics stimulates the best part of me (my brain—let's focus) and leaves me invigorated—even if the conversation is arduous.

I wish I wrote more about how safe I feel in your arms at night. And about how I can't get close enough to you, even when I only leave you an inch or two to sleep on. And how secure I feel when I reach over and you're actually there. My heart fills and I can rest and leave my worries behind knowing I'm safe and you'll keep watch. Because I know you've got me.

I wish I could look into your eyes every day, even if I did blush and drop my gaze. Feel your skin on mine, your hands on the back of my neck and your teeth and kisses on the front. And about how that thought alone gets me hot and bothered and makes me shiver all at once.

I wish you knew that you're one of my first thoughts in the morning and one of the last at night. I wish I could express how I finally understand what that all-too-often-used cliché feels like and actually means. I wish I could tell you how much I miss you and how much I care and how big a part of my life you really are. Because I don't think you know. And I certainly don't think I tell you enough.

I wish I told you more. Held you more. Hugged you more. Ran my fingers up the back of your neck more. Kissed you more. Made love to you more. And fell asleep next to you more. I wish there were more opportunities to put my head on that spot, my spot, on your chest and snuggle down with you more. And just be.

Just once more.

At Night

Every time I close my eyes
I see you
I can feel your breath
On my neck
Your arms around my waist
Your hands holding mine
There's no reprieve from you
Even in my dreams

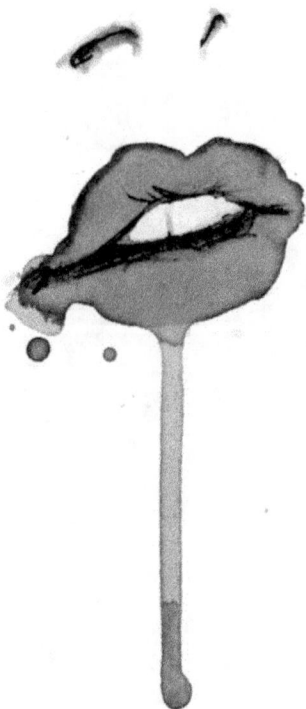

Smile for Me

I miss
That smile.
The one
You smile
Where you turn up
Just one corner
Of your mouth
And then the next.

The one where
Your eyebrows raise
Just a hint
And
Your eyes light up
At the sight of me
Catching you
Watching me.

The one that
Adores me
Somehow
For whatever
Unknown reason.

The one
That answers
All the questions
Unasked
Or untold.

I miss
The smile
You smile
With your eyes.
Because
As much
As I adore

Your lips,
Your eyes
Never lie.

Missing Home

I miss the home I've made with you.
The spot on your chest
That was made for my head
To rest
(Rest...)
And my hand on your heart
Just listening to you breathe
(Breathe. Breathe. Breathe.)
Slowly,
As you drift too.

Inside your arms
A sanctuary exists.
It's my home alone
And no one else matters here.
There is no alternate world—
No other universe.

I can breathe you in
And sink into you
Until we become me
And I become you
And us becomes one.

Here there is safety.
Here there is home.
Here in this bubble
Like a candy-coated shell
Strong and sweet, yet fragile
No worries exist but the
Dawning of the last sunrise together.

And it's days like these I'm sad to see the sun,
Melting the sugar-coated candy nighttime away.

So, So Long

My fingers have forgotten what you taste like;
You've been gone so long.

Safe Space

Please be my safe space tonight.

The place I can rest and you hold me with arms strong and gentle.
Where the world fades away,
And
At least for a little while,
I don't have to be vigilant,
Or strong.

Where I can melt into you
For what will simultaneously feel
Like a second
And all eternity.

Where I know
You
Will protect me
And my heart
From all the world's troubles.

A space so quiet and sacred
That I know the heartbeats
I hear are filled with love—
And never fear.

A space so safe that for once
I can actually breathe
And finally
Truly
Quietly
And peacefully
Rest.

So that when the welcomed but dreaded sun should rise
You can see
In my eyes
The stillness
And calm

And comfort
Of finally having been home.

Missing Piece

I miss you so badly it hurts.
The missing and the wanting
And the needing to be close.
It runs so deep it aches.

And the hard part is that
I know if I had you here today
It still wouldn't be enough.
If I could touch and smell and taste and hold you
It would quell that pain but only for a while.

Because whether I had you for an hour, a day, a week, or a month, it still
wouldn't matter.
It's never enough.
In the end you must leave.

And I always end up
Alone.

High

I miss the high I get from you.
I miss your touch. Your kiss.
I miss you holding me.
I miss the butterflies I get waiting for you to arrive.
I miss smiling and laughing so hard it hurts.
I miss the silly jokes and the stupid conversations and the late nights
that turn into deliciously late nights.

You're an addiction I will not be cured of.
I miss your high.

12 Months

I love having you in my life.
I want more of you in my life.
I want to wake up next to you.
I love the way you "get" me; but I also love the way you think you understand everything about you, about us, about life, about the way the world works.
I love watching you talk about the things you absolutely adore; you light up and you don't even know it.
I love your smile and I love the way your smile makes me smile. Every time.
I love your skin, and my fingers on your skin.
And although I'm not naive enough to believe that life is dreadfully simple, if I had 12 months to live, I'd choose you as my person.

Tomorrow

When you walk
Through the door
My hands rest gently
On your chest,
Up to your shoulders,
Around the back of your neck,
And pull you close
With a kiss; hello;
Welcome home, my love.

You finally let go
Of the day
Of the struggles
The wins
The losses.
You tell me about everything
That went right
And the few things that
Maybe went wrong.

I hand you a drink
While we sit and talk
And you rub my feet.

That's the tomorrow
I long for.

To welcome you home
With a kiss
Hello.

To be the place
You come home to.

Without

Your scent on my pillow.
I squeeze it tighter.
It lingers.
I miss you already.
.

.

.

The warmth in my bed,
The heat from your body
Makes it hard to sleep.
Difficult to acclimate to
In fits and short bursts.
But I'd take one hundred thousand
Sleepless nights
Just to lay next to you.
Just to know you're here.

The night broken up,
Paused,
By the constant checking
Touching
Reaching
Feeling
Ensuring
Confirming
We're still here.
Together.
.

.

.

I wish
We had a place
We didn't have to learn
To live without.

I wish
We had a place
Where living with
Wasn't the thing
We had to get used to.

Lip Sync Journey

I wish you were here so I could give you kisses. On your forehead. The bridge and tip of your nose. That tiny spot under your eye. I would line your cheek with flutters. Up toward your ear and on it so that you just make out the soft sound of my lips parting to shower you tenderly with love. The sweet spot behind and just beneath your ear now. Down your neck to find and gently dot your collarbone. Out then, tracing the ridge it makes up, and back in again. Slowly on their journey. Then up the front of your neck and throat, resting easy on your chin. Until finally my lips find their way to yours, but—pausing there as if to recoup from the trek and catch a breath—they curl upwards, in awe and wonderment and joyous splendor for their homecoming. Lingering patiently there as our eyelashes embrace in a dance of warm and sweet hellos. My hand finds your cheek and strokes it softly. My smile sneaks through as I see past your eyes. Everything is still. Everything is calm in the quiet, timeless void between heartbeats. Until, uproariously and in an instant, you welcome me home, and take my breath away...

Thāt Kïss

I miss your kiss.

The kiss you kiss me with
When you sweep your thumb
Across my face
And hold the back of my neck
With your strong hand
And pull me in close with the other
And your lips meet mine
And you exhale
And relax into me
And it's just me and you
You and me
Home finally

Thāt Kïss.

Beacon

My heart
Waits for yours
Like a beacon
In the night.
Ever ready
To guide you back home.

I Wish

I wish I could touch you.
I wish I could see you more.
I wish you were closer.
I wish I could kiss your neck
And rub your temples when you come home.

I wish there was more me and you,
And less the world and everyone else.

Come Back to Bed

The scent of you lingers
On the sheets that miss you too.

Aching, Longing, Hoping, Waiting

My heart aches for you...
My mind aches for the fun, funny, silly and sometimes ridiculous
conversations that kept us either laughing, debating, or both.
I wait in angst to see your phenomenal smile; your happiness fills my
heart and makes it radiate joy.
My waist aches for the safety of your arms to wrap me up and pull me
close.
The back of my neck for the gentle pull of your fingertips and palm of
your hand.
My collarbones for your kisses.
My neck for your lips.

Every day I miss you like this.

My fingertips ache for your arms, your shoulders, and the back of your
neck.
My skin aches for the warmth of your body;
I miss the warmth of you in more ways than one.
I ache for the way you excite my skin and make me shiver with one
precisely placed touch of your lips.
I ache for the pressure on my hips that inevitably makes me give in and
give up the indistinguishable sound that lets you know I am yours alone.
I long for the moment I can finally melt into you, like I do, and have
done, for no other.

I miss being next to you.
Draping my legs over you.
The sanctuary of being curled up in your arms.
The smallness I feel when tucked neatly into you;
An actual speck of dust in the universe, and you my protective shell.
I miss the smell of you,
The taste of you.

But so much more than any of this, I long to wake up next to you, aching
no more.

In My Head

Fucking with my mind
From hundreds of miles away...

All I want is you.

Come to my rescue
Or stop destroying me.

...Sweetie

Sadness welled in her eyes
As she thought of the future.

The what-ifs, the could-have-beens,
The might-bes, the don'ts.
The maybe-just-becauses
And the maybe-we-won'ts.

What will never come to pass
Is the scariest thing we'll see.
Imagination running wild
And reckless
And altogether too free.

Just then
He spoke

Returning her silence
And calming that raging sea.
He stopped all time
Filled her lungs with breath
And arrested her anxiety

When
With
A
Single
Word
He called out to her...

Ways and Means

I keep searching for ways
To make myself not love you.

Reasons to convince myself
It doesn't mean what I think it does.

Things that should indicate to me
That it's just not meant to be.

That what I feel is silly, foolish, naive.
Ridiculous and a result of circumstance.

Things that should direct my thoughts and feelings
Toward the inverse of what they are today.

Age.
Distance.
Timing;
- Time here.
- Time gone.
- Time between now and what could one day be.
Status, stature, state;
- Of being
- Of mind
- Of body
- Of sound spirit.
Health.
Experience.
Position.
Wealth;
- That which is innate,
- That which is learned,
- And that which is earned.
Familiarity;
- And that which is foreign.
The lives that came before,
- To which I'll never have insight.

The lives that are,
And the ones that will never be.

Yet,

Despite all the things I think should lead me away—
The ways I try to find to invalidate what I feel—
That what I feel is not really what it means—
I find my heart returning home
To the place it knows
And has known
And has waited for.

Home to you.
Foolishly, perhaps,
And by any means.

The Thing About Emotions... // Conversations at Midnight

Sometimes I'm too much of a realist.

Always you are.
I don't think you're trying to protect yourself in this case.

A lack of emotion works against me sometimes.

I don't think you have a lack of emotion.

The people who seem to have a lack of emotion feel the most.
And love the hardest, and hurt the deepest, too.

That's why there's that wall.
It's not a lack of emotion. It's a convergence of too much emotion.
Too much to process. So, it gets turned off and we act like we don't care.

What she said...

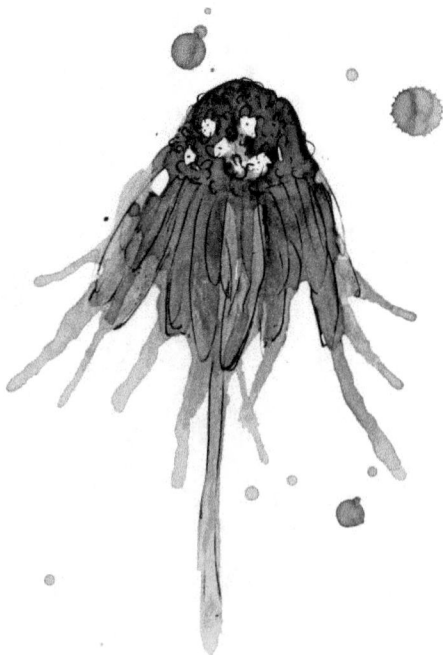

Make The World Go Away

I miss you
I miss your smart mouth
I miss your laugh
I miss your smile
I miss your hands
I miss your body
I miss the feel of your body
In my hands.
I miss your fingers on my neck
And back.
The feel of your shoulders
Under my fingertips.
Your lips on my mouth.
That very distinct way
You make me feel
When the whole world
Disappears.

I miss you making the world disappear.

Come home
And make the world

Disappear.

In this World and the Next

In you, I've found my one true love.
The essence my heart has waited for forever.
I love you with my whole soul
And will continue to love you forever.

I want to hold your hand
And scratch your head
And rub your neck when you come home.
Kiss you softly and squeeze you close.
I want to be the safe, soft place you can land.

I want to be your confidant
Your companion
Your champion and cheering squad
And, of course,
The one razzing you
About this and about that
And about everything in between.

I want to build dreams with you
Make new days with you
Discover new things,
    Small and insignificant;
    Large and maybe even mediocre.
I want it to be you that I make mistakes with.
I want to fight and make up,
Laugh and cry and say I'm sorry.

I love you so deeply
It hurts.
    I now know
    Where the very bottom of my soul
    Resides.
I miss you so dearly
It aches even when you're near me.

I now understand how

Jennifer Derby

Words could never be enough.
For my soul is tethered to yours
In this lifetime
And, hopefully, the next.
But surely in the ones that came before them.

I hope you'll wait for me.
Or I for you.
So that someday,
In a space and time that transcends the physical,
In a world where days and months and years and time do not exist,
In a place where the lost are found
And the restless no longer travel alone
We can someday
Be together.

For it was always you my heart waited for.
And it will always be you my heart returns home to.

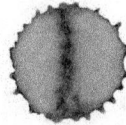

ACT III: The Aching

Indifference

The hardest part is that
It's serious
But casual.

Love is a Liar

- **"I'll make you feel good"**
- *But Love, all I feel is aching.*

- **"I'll never leave you lonely"**
- *But Love, all I feel is alone.*

- **"You'll never want for love"**
- *But Love, all I feel is yearning.*

- **"I'll be there for you always"**
- *But Love, I have no one at all.*

- **"I'll make you happy"**
- *But Love, all I feel are tears.*

- **"I'll hold your heart"**
- *But Love, all I feel is broken.*

- **"I'll make you confident"**
- *But Love, I never seem sure.*

- **"I'll hold you up"**
- *But Love, there are no hands to catch me as I fall.*

- **"I'll put your first"**
- *But Love, I'm last on your list.*

- **"I'll lay with you each night"**
- *But Love, half the bedclothes are cold.*

- **"I'll show you the world"**
- *But Love, I'm stuck in a daydream.*

- **"I'll give you everything"**
- *But Love, I get nothing at all.*

- **"I'll never hurt you"**

- *But Love,*
- **"I promise"**
- *But Love,*
- **"Don't you believe me?"**
- *I do. I mean, I want to.*
- **"Trust me"**
- *But Love,*
- **"Trust me"**
- *But, my Love, you've already destroyed me. One thousand times one thousand times one thousand times over.*
- **"I swear this to you"**
- *But Love, my Sweet Love, you are nothing but a romancer. I fear, My Love, you are a teller of lies.*

Waiting

I feel like
I'm just waiting
For something
Someone
That will never come.

The simple touch
Of a passing hand.
A hug from behind.
A kiss on the neck.
The smell of you.
The softness of your shirt
As I nestle into you.

Just the feeling of your fingers
Running up and down my back
And your breath on my neck

A touch
A kiss
A word
A

Jennifer Derby

Timing

Why are the best relationships
The ones you never saw coming?

Why do you fall hardest
For the ones you can never reach?

Why are the happiest relationships
The ones you can't be in?

Why can you love someone so much
Know everything about your life is right
And never be with that person?

Why can you love me in the dark
But never even slightly in the light?

Why can't I feel your touch at night
When I most need you near me?

Why aren't you here when I'm down
To pick me up and help me rise?

Why do I find myself in the right story
At precisely the wrong time?

Goodnight My Love

I still reserve
Your side of the bed
Even though
I know
It will probably
Never
Be filled
With the
Warmth
Of
You.

Hurting

You're crushing me
And you don't even know it.
I'm hurting so much
But you can't even see it.

You may think of me occasionally
But I'm more of an afterthought.
I hear your words
But I cannot feel what they mean.

I know you think about me
And the things you should probably do
But I don't seem to mean enough to you
And so you stop just short of taking action.

I'm hurt and I'm angry
But more than that I'm disappointed.
And I'm not even as disappointed in you
As I am in myself
For letting you treat me this way.

I hope you are able to reconcile your feelings
And be honest with yourself
And then with me.
Because I'm better than this.
And I deserve more.

Show Me

Don't tell me you love me.
Don't tell me you care.
Don't tell me it's alright.
Don't tell me it's fair.

Don't tell me all the things you think you should.
The "here's-how-it-wills" and the "here's-how-we-coulds".
The "Baby-one-day-we-will-rule-the-world".
The "just-hold-on-a-while-and-you'll-be-my-girl."

The should-haves, the could-haves, the want-tos, the nots.
These words that you spew do not mean a lot.

Instead
Show me the way you feel for me.
Show me the love you've concealed for me.
Show me the way you've always longed to express
Show me the desire that will crack open my chest.

Reach the inside of me
Without all the talk
Reach the inside of me
While walking the walk

Show me all the things that you speak of.
Show me the depth of your so-called love.

The Heart of Change

Can you ever really lose something
You never had to begin with...?

You pulled me in
And I caved.
Wasn't hard, really.
You were so very much
What I wanted;
What I needed;
What I craved.

I pulled you in
Because...
I wouldn't let go;
Not you. Not this time.
You tried—
Not emphatically—
But I wouldn't let you
Take the easy way out.
It took but a touch
A genuine and gentle stroke, my Darling
To make you stay.

You wanted to feel,
And I
Wanted
You.
And you knew that spark
Was different.

I pressed just so.
No need for cunning
Or calculated manipulation.
No need to convince.
No need to deceive.
It was easy,
Effortless,

To be truly me,
Every day
With you.

And I think that for you
It was easy
To take
Everything—
As much as I gave away—
So freely.
Not maliciously.
But wantonly. And lasciviously.

Even so
I never really got all of you.
More than many, perhaps.
And, still now, likely more than most.
But not enough for
Real
Lasting and
Meaningful
Change.

Not this time.

This space is the heart of change.
But we drift. Limbo. Stasis.
Suspension. Holding.
Certain uncertainty.

And so we find ourselves—
Or, maybe, I find myself—
Living in another reality.
Unwilling to accept
The fate of this world.

Naive, maybe.
Unwilling to see, perhaps.
Pretending it's enough, sure.

Jennifer Derby

Shrugging it off as if it's no big deal, more than often.
But blind, never.

It still hurts,
Inside,
Where I am tremendously skilled
At keeping things out of the light.
It stabs much more deeply
Than any one person could understand.
It burns in my chest
As I feel it caving in.
Shallows my breathing,
And raises my anxiety,
The thought of losing you.

And somehow, ironically,
Though the thought is strikingly painful
It's as if I have no place to feel that pain.

So where are we?
Are we?

And can you ever really lose something
That wasn't ever yours to begin with...?

Evolve it. Or dissolve it.

With you
I simultaneously
Feel like the luckiest
And unluckiest
Person
In the world.

And Yet...

She loved him.
She was sure.
And he, her.

It was true.
And he cared.
Felt more than he should.

She could see
Into his soul.
And he could
Shake her world.

And yet,
As sure as the sunset
Gave way to darkness
Every night
She found herself
Alone.

She loved him.
She was sure.
But he
Couldn't love her.

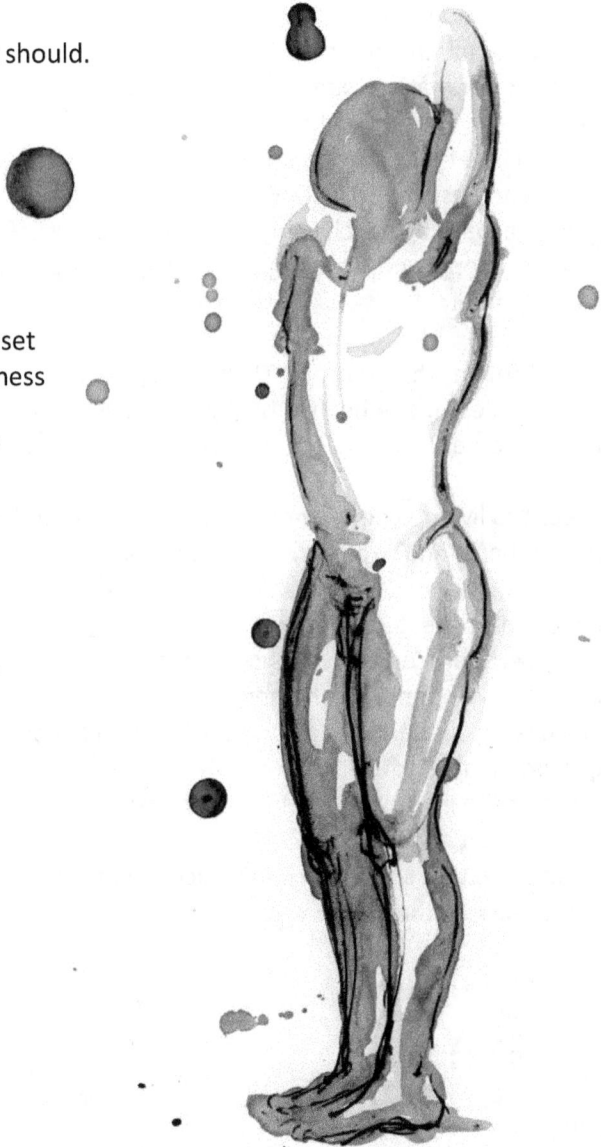

Fairytales & Lies

But it wouldn't work, would it?
We don't want the perfect life.
The one laid out in fairytales.
The happily-ever-afters.

We want passion. We want lust. We want fullness.
And shivers running down our spine.
We want our breath stolen
And the rest of the world to fall away
As we fall into the arms of a lover.
We want an absence so distant it aches.
We want a wanting which cannot be satiated.
We want to long, and, the longer we long, the higher the high when
finally we meet.

And that touch. That warmth. That energy.
That breathlessness when we finally meet eye to eye, and tongue to
tongue, and our lips taste that sweet familiar that will not, cannot, be
forgotten.
We want to live off the memory of the last time our bodies were tangled
into one. Bare. And exposed. And vulnerable.

But we can't have it all.
And we certainly can't have it both ways.
We can't have happily-ever-after,
And a passion so fierce it could spark fire with the static electricity of a
single well-placed touch.
We can't have incredible, intense, and heated love-making year after
year after year after year.
We can't feel that spark and ignite such a flame without the drudgery of
the everyday getting in the way.

We can't have a fantasy
And a reality
That perfectly align...

...Can we?

Why; Not Enough

Why won't you let me love you?
Why won't you even let me try?
What are you so afraid of?
Is it because you don't want to leave me when you die?

Or is it because of "what they'll all say"
Or they way they'll gawk and gossip
I've given everything to you for years
But you keep slipping through my fingers and there, again, I've lost it.

Can never be close in the way we want
Can never share the important things
There's a fissure between us where my happiness fades
Because I know the life we're living some call sin

You won't let me in
Even with every gentle touch
I can't win with you
And it's taking too much

Just please tell me where I stand
Just please let me in
I'm begging; why won't you let me love you?
Why can't you let our love win?

After all these years of searching,
I think I've finally found
The one who steals my breath away
And makes my heavy heart pound.

Yet, here we are
In this same place once again
In this in-between, this somethingness
Why can't you let our love win?

All I want is to be one,
Not these separate and distinct two

Why won't you let me get close?
Why am I not enough to you?

I'm consumed with you. Every moment. I share everything with you. Whether you're here or far away.

All the little things, the big things, anything in my life with meaning. If it means something to me, I share it with you. Conversations in my head that never actually come true. Parts of my life I wish you had a part in. Maybe had an influence on.

It's not an obsession or a compulsion, but rather a longing, a desire, a yearning to have you close. Close to my skin. Close to my lips. Close to my heart. Despite my want, you're still so far away.

I hate these walls. These societal norms that keep us apart. Boundaries that stop our love from being all we know it could be. It's not even the distance so much as the cloaks we live under. Some days, the weight of the darkness is crushing.

I know better. You don't want me like I want you. I'm not enough, and still I stay. Somehow holding out a small but simple sliver of hope that someday it just might happen.

Your Other Life

I wish I knew
The part of you
I'll never get to see

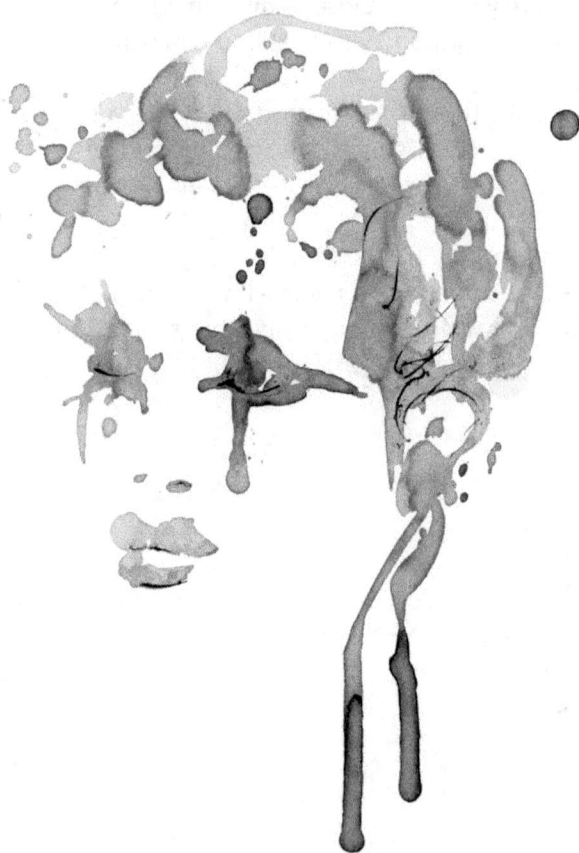

Jennifer Derby

Handle with Care

This whole thing is getting harder.
Every day I wake up more and more forlorn.
Worse than the day before.
I feel like my heart is crumbling
Into a million tiny pieces
Being carried away like dust in the wind.

Why did I give away so much power?
Why did I let you hold me together?
Why did I give you my heart to keep safe?
Don't you realize how important that is?
How difficult that was for me to do?
Why aren't you more careful with these fragile things?

Day at the Beach

I was the sunshine in your day.
The warmth that kissed your face.
The light that brightened even your darkest crevices, softened your
spirit, melted your mood, and soothed your soul.

I was the feeling of soft, white sand beneath your feet and between
your toes.
The sea water lapping up ever so sweetly, gently, tenderly onto the
land. My waves washing up with the softest touch, receding with the
gentlest stroke.

I was the ocean breeze caressing all of you, whisking your troubles
away. I was a place of refuge. A place to recharge. A place you could
come to, to get away from the world. Just me and you. You and the
ocean breeze.

I was the salt air you could breathe in and close your eyes and know you
were home.

Why?
Why did you stay away?
Why wouldn't you come home?
Why did you let me love you like that?
Let me give you all of me?
Why didn't you tell me
You didn't prefer the sand?
Why didn't you tell me
You were a mountain man?

The In-Between

Love on the edge
There in the in-between;
That space
After one breath ends
Before the other begins
That void is where our love hangs
Suspended.

There are no yesterdays
There are no tomorrows
There are no absolutes.
There is no concreteness
To hold fast to.
There are no stories
To be shared,
Or foundations
To be built upon.
No pictures,
Or memories.
There are only right-nows.
Here in the in-between.

We're not quite in
And we're not quite out.
We're not quite here
And we're not quite there.
We are—in fact—nowhere
And everywhere
All at once.

We hold fast
To two worlds;
If only we could somehow
Turn them into
One.
There is no us
There is no "them".

There's just you
Wanting a girl you won't have;
And me
Wanting a man I can't.

It's tricky—
Walking that fine line
Between where one life ends
And the other begins.
Intertwined,
Yet segregated.
Together, yet
So alone.

Not quite shared
Not quite connected
Not quite woven
Into one.
But messy,
And jagged,
And painful.

Mostly, though,
It's lonely
Being so close together
And yet so far apart.

I wonder if,
Somehow,
Someday,
Somewhere,
We'll be able to breathe
Together.
Instead of balancing our love
On a sliver
There in the in-between.

Work > Me

My heart is hurting
All over
Again.
I'm tired.
And anxious.
And through.
Spent.

I've fought too many battles
And haven't won enough wars.
And it feels like I've gotten up
Just one too many times.

My heart is crumbling
All over
Again.
I can't breathe.
And I feel the pain, sharp as a knife,
Cut through my very
Soul.

I can feel it coming.
I can see clearly what's happening.
You knew that taking one thing meant
Losing another.

You took it anyway.

Chose the only way
You knew how to choose.
Once again.
But this time,
Instead
Of doing the dirty work yourself
You thought
It'll play itself out
Just like I want it to.

Just as you convinced yourself
"It should".

You knew distance would close in
And familiarity would complicate things.
And inevitably and invariably
There would come a time
When
It just wouldn't work well
Anymore.

Chose work
Over hard work.

And so,
Ironically,
Instead of writing your story
You chose the path that let life dictate the narrative for you.

Only this time
Was different.
Because this time
She loved you.

She loved you with a patience unmatched
And a heart so grand
It overflowed.
A heart that loved you for you.
A heart that was stubborn
And gracious,
Forgiving
And fierce.
Strong
And willing.

And
And
And...

You
Loved
Her
Too.

Still—
You chose the path that offered you
Everything,
Except
The one thing you
Needed,
Longed for,
Could not buy,
And cannot force.

Again.

Give Away

I gave away my power.
Because you're such the alpha
I've been longing for.
I gave you too much.

Too much of me
Too much of my strength
Too much compassion
Keeping little to nothing
For myself.

Gave you too much influence.
Became blind.
Didn't see what I was doing to myself.
I gave you far too much control.

On the outside
You'd never know.
On the inside
I'm suffering.
But this
Is mostly
Of my own doing.

I know better now.
I'm learning.
I've got a ways to go,
But you've helped me to notice
How much of myself I was still giving away.

Just the What-Ifs

So tell me
Am I just a thing to make you feel good?
A thing that helps you feel alive?
A warm body to fulfill some basic human tactile need?

I think I fit in that space.
Sure.
But I also think I bleed slightly outside those lines
Into a realm you weren't expecting me to occupy.

A complicated and awkward space, to be certain.
But a space that makes you question
Where we are
What we are
Who we are.
Is this it? Is this the thing we're supposed to be?

What if
We could have been more?
What if timing was perfect?
What if you could have been with the person you love;
The one you fit with
And the one you belong to?

Would it be any easier?
Or would there just be different challenges?
What's it worth?
What do we have left?
What do we really have to lose?
What's at stake?

How long will we be content to just
Occupy the time?

Not surprisingly, that same damned what-if
Wonders if
Maybe

Something
Will allow the stars to align.

What if they could?
What then?

There in the Dark Place

There's a chasm.
A distance.
An uneasiness.
A tension.
There is a friction
Somewhere between us.

We don't speak of it.
Never bring it up.
But we feel it,
And we know
We are one step away
From hurt
Neither of us wants to feel.

We go about our days
With casual *I love yous*
Eyes-wide-open meaningless kisses
Smiling with our mouths
But never our eyes.

Hiding the hurt
We sleep like strangers.
Touch like friends.
And talk like business partners
Conducting transactions.

We make love in much the same way
Except
There is no
Real love
Left to be made.

We find no sense in being sensual.
No comfort in holding hands.
Cold feet no longer
Warm beneath the other's legs in bed.

The distance floats between us
Like icebergs in the Bering sea.
Harsh and jagged and frigid.
We don't dare explore
What lies beneath the surface.

Breaking apart at the seams,
Our love melting
And watered down,
We grasp onto anything
In the darkness,
Hoping, perhaps,
To find our way
Back to the light.

There's a rift.
A hurting.
A pain between us.
A void left
By the blunt ends of our heartstrings
Cut harshly, and way too soon.
Unraveling,
This empty space
Now overflows with hidden
But not so secret pain.

Let Go

I've left you
One thousand times
In my mind.

And yet
I cannot
Let
You
Go

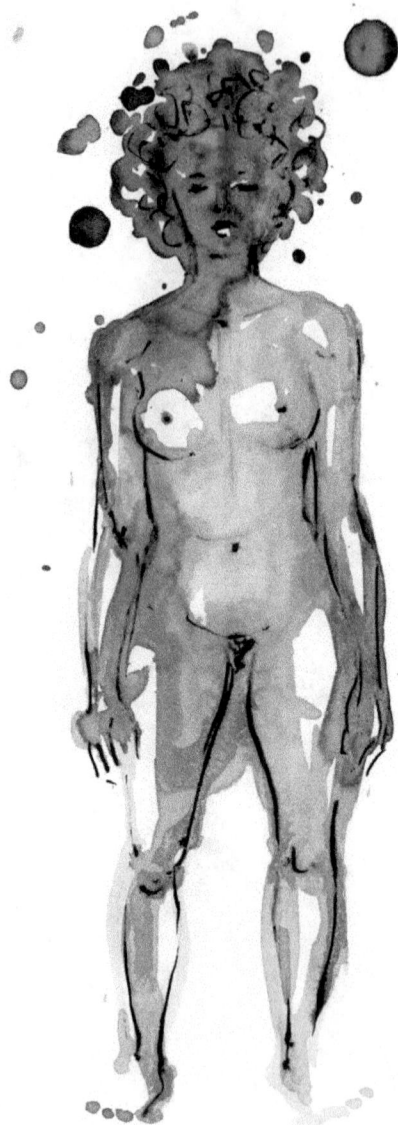

ACT IV: The Leaving

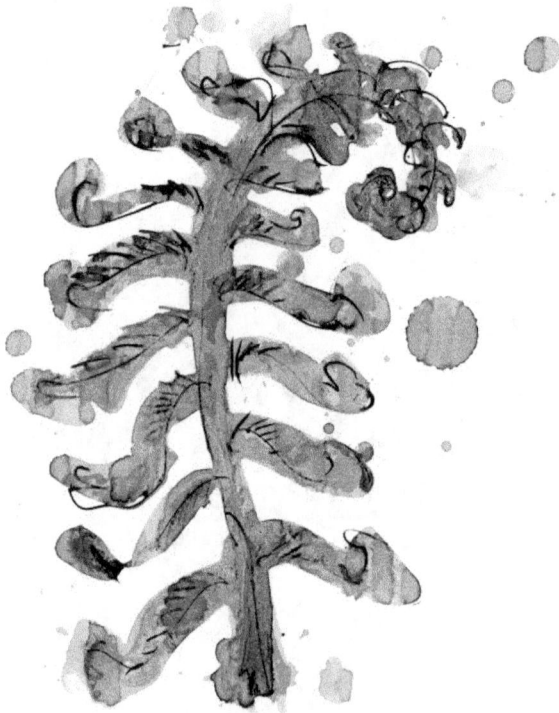

I need to say goodbye to you.
But I can't decide
If staying hurts more
Than leaving will.

Goodbye

I need to say goodbye to you
I promise you that it is the very last thing
My heart wants.
But in my head,
I know it's time.

Time to free you of that place.
Of finding a reason to come back to me
Every so often.
Free you and also myself
Of all the feelings of guilt.
Free us of the hurt
And free myself of the sliver of hope
That keeps me holding on to you.

Some days I feel as if my heart is a balloon
That follows you around
And my heartstring leans ever close to you
No matter where you go,
And no matter how far.
But you just won't turn around and grab that damned string.

And perhaps in the meantime
There are others just admiring that balloon
Wishing they could get the chance to hold it close
Even if only for a moment.
But being tethered to you
Doesn't allow me to see the world around me
Or let others in.
I'm walled off from seeing the good intentions of a would-be suitor, or
even just a potential friend.

You were there for me when my world fell apart
And helped me realize that I could put it back together again.

With you, I've learned so much about myself.
You've taught me that I'm not broken.

That I can love and love unconditionally
And I can trust another.
That I'm a little bit of a fool sometimes.
And that I'm stronger than I had imagined.
That I can care for another.
And that it's ok to be vulnerable
Even when it's scary.
That I am worthy of love
And that I am worthy of more.

When I'm with you
You are everything to me.
The innocence in your smile
Makes me smile—every time.
When I look into your eyes
I can feel the way you love me,
But also the way you want to,
And the way you can't.

So I need to say goodbye to you.
I promise you it's the very last thing
My heart wants.
But in my head,
I know it's time.

I Should Go

I love you—
But I'm not supposed to.

I miss you—
But I shouldn't.

I know better—
But something pulls me back to you.

You belong to someone else.
You don't treat me like you should.
I don't hear "I'll try"
Or "I'll leave" or "It will be better soon".

And I know I should go
I should just walk away.
But I've also never felt
A connection like ours before.

But
I must remember myself in it all.
And not compromise myself again.
So, as hard as it will be to let you go,
I know
The you that is here is not good for me.

And if I have to miss you
So that I may be whole,
I'll miss you dearly.
But never desperately
Again.

Finding A Way To Say Goodbye

"Hey baby, how was your day?"
"I'm good. Long day. Just trying to find a way to say goodbye to you."

That's what I want to say. Not really *wanting* to say anything, but wanting to make it easier for you.

I knew you were tired tonight. Had had a long exhausting day. And I pushed you anyway. Sometimes that's the only way I can get emotion out of you. And truth. When you're tired and you've no defenses or wit or smart-assery left.

-Why do you stay?
-Why won't you leave?
-Why is this so hard?
-Are you just waiting for one of us to leave you first?

Invariably, I got my answers. And I'm as disappointed as I am satisfied, because I know you and I knew what I would get. I know all the reasons. You're too old. You've got less than half a lifetime left. You two don't fight, things aren't bad, they're just not good. It would never work. I'm just starting out this lifetime and I wouldn't understand. I can't understand until I'm left with less than half a lifetime.

I pushed you and you gave me exactly what I expected. You're tired. You've been through it before. It's hard and it's stressful and none of it is fun. You've built up your life again out of nothing, twice over. To break that down now, you'd be left with half of everything. So you stay. Things aren't good. They're just not horrible.

You're blocking my life and interfering. You think you're even making me sick. Stopping my life from progressing this way or that. Too complicated. What about this, and what about that, and what about the other?

Yes, I hate it too. I hate being that person. In the middle. In the in-between. The one who is and who isn't all at once. The omnipresent and the invisible. That's who I am. I don't like it, but I've somehow managed

115

to settle into this uncomfortable space. Loving a man who can't or won't love me back. Not the way I'll ever want him to. Not the way he wants to. Not the way either of us imagined it.

When you find the right person at the wrong time, everything seems to go to hell. So you've got to decide: will you go to hell, too? Will you go through hell for the one you say you love? How much hell is too much? Is there just a right amount? Have we reached our thresholds?

I know all the reasons it won't work. But am I too much a dreamer for believing in the one reason it would?
Maybe.
Maybe I am that foolish to think that love cures all and heals all and ultimately perseveres. That love saves all. And love will make it all work.

Maybe this life just isn't wired to work that way. Maybe TV and fairytales have us all fooled. Maybe,
Maybe
It's
just
time
to say
goodbye.

I love you. But I'm no good for you. I've only made things harder, despite being a soft place to land. I'm sorry I wasn't enough for you. I'm sorry you let yourself believe that I was. But I'm not. I'm just a distraction. I'm a good time. And a confidant. And a place to feel good. But I can't be more than these things.

And so, for this reason, I'll make the choice for you. And for me. And I will let you go. And I can stop missing you. And I can stop hurting, too. I can stop waiting. And waiting. And waiting. For what I know will never come. Grow old waiting on a man who'll never have me. The world just doesn't work that way.

It's an impossible situation really. We got here innocently enough. But maybe we held on too long? Maybe I should have let you walk away. I'm not really a part of your life. And I guess you're not really a part of mine.

Maybe this will free you. Of that place. Stop trying to find things that lead you back here. That's no way to hold on to a person.

You're at a place in your life where you don't want to do it again. Have to rebuild again. Give up half of what you have now and start over. Again. Just settling in, and having to upset the apple cart. Again. Too old. Having come too far. And really just very tired.

Too tired to do it all again.

I get it.
And I'm just not enough.
I get that, too.

So I'll say the things I've been meaning to say. The things I've thought to say a thousand times a thousand times a thousand times before.

I can't do this any longer. We can't do this any longer. We're hurting one another. Indirectly, but it still hurts. I can't sit and wait for you to not make decisions any longer. I can't sit here pretending that, one day, everything is going to change. That we'll build a life together. That that happily-ever-after's actually going to come true.

I can't be this "other" any longer. I'm more than that. And I know my worth. But I've been selling myself short all these years. For you. And now I feel stupid. And foolish. And used. And worthless.

For loving a man I couldn't choose not to love any longer.

Rush-hour Daydreams

Red-faced from the light,
Bloodshot eyes,
Salt-laced streaks,
And messy mascara
Where tears once ran.

.

Most days
She's ok now.
But there are still those
In which
Not all time passes
So effortlessly,
With forgiveness,
And without detection.

.

There are still some
Wherein life pauses
In a place—
Not of her choosing—
And in those moments
She is powerless
To the force that draws her
To sit still and wander.

.

She drifts away
To the sounds rushing past her;
Once again in a daydream
Her heart ached to fall back into...

.

Holding hands,
Laughing
With a laugh that
Could only
Be felt in the depth
Of your being;
The laughter that
Brought tears

Because it felt so, so good.

.

The softest,
Sweetest kisses
Stolen
As she leaned over
The center console
And placed them
Tenderly on his ear.

.

Where words were left unspoken
Because the eyes said it all.
And where the feeling of fingertips
On goose-bumped skin
Was the most
Amazingly heightened sense
On the face of the earth.

.

They were each
The other's soul;
The only ones who understood—
The only real connection
In a world otherwise hidden behind
6x3 inch liquid crystal walls.

.

Alas
He could not come
Nor would he be able to stay
And the world they'd built
Together
Would crumble
Under the weight of a world
Closing in on them from outside.
It would not be as forgiving
As it had been
In these tiny
Preciously-captured
Capsules of time

.

She was so lost
She didn't even notice
The flicker of the light
From red to green
Until the horns barked abruptly behind her
And startled her out of her
Dreamlike haze.

.

And in that moment she did
The only thing she knew to do.
With a calm, determined focus
She came back to the world
Zipped up her heart
In its stone-cold exterior
Wiped the past from her cheeks
And kept driving forward.

Alone

Life has a strange way
Of teaching you about yourself

You've always felt a little alone;
But now life lets you choose.

Would you rather be alone with a man who loves you?
Alone with a man who can't?
Or alone with a man who sometimes wants you, but only in the
shallowest sense?

What kind of aloneness do you prefer?
Which kind of alone will you choose?

Sis, for all this talk of being alone,
Why look outside for your worth?

How about learning to be ok
Being alone with you?

We Ruined Me

I deserted myself
In my haste to love you.
Scarred and damaged,
Black and blue,
Purple and green,
Bloodied and bruised.
Used up and empty.
Hurting from hurts that came long before
And drenched in brokenness and pain.
I abandoned myself to love you.
Because, even though
You couldn't love me back—
Not the way that I yearned for
And not the way that we wanted—
That pain stabbed so deeply
That there, buried in the darkness,
I finally felt something.
And it had been so long
Since I'd felt anything at all,
That feeling you not loving me—
And me letting you—
Still felt so good.

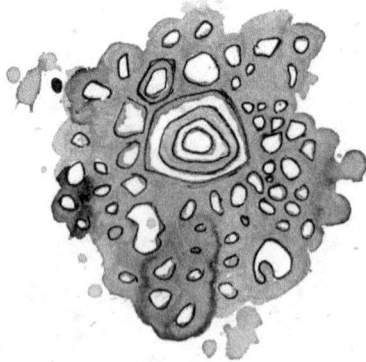

Jennifer Derby

Before You Go

So kiss me once before you go
Remind me of that place I used to know
Where we loved and laughed
And made believe
We had everything we needed
Kiss me once before you go
Remind me of that time when we both knew
We were meant for each other
We'd conquer the world
You were my man and I was your girl

Kiss me once before you go
Remind me of that place we used to know
Where we laughed and loved
Stayed up till the sun
Pretending our love
Could overcome
Every roadblock they threw at us,
Put in our way
Hoping our love
Would always stay

We were safe in the dark
But not around town
Where our so-called friends
Tried to tear us down
They'd talk and they'd whisper
Side-eye, disapprove
Stomp out our flame
Like a cigarette under shoe
The pressure too great
For our now fragile embers
The world was too harsh
To let us remember
That first time we touched
The goosebumps, our first kiss
The way you held me softly

Our first night of bliss
Our heart-pounding love
That made us feel alive
The sweet but simple pleasure
Of just looking in your eyes
Our hours of conversation
Silly, serious, and in-between
I'd implore you to stay up talking
But sleep would always win
The way you'd hold me close
My head on your shoulder
We'd dance long after
The music was over

So kiss me once more before you go
Help me forget what the world had in store
Forcing the notion that our love didn't conform
To what this world
Considered its norm

Battered and withered
The world sucked us dry
Till they got what they wanted
And we let our love die

Love you - G'Night

I don't know if you'll
Get to a point
Where
You'll let yourself
Believe you're
Deserving of love
I don't know if you'll get to the place
Where
You ever really let me
Love you
But either way
I'll be here
Ready to love you
When you're ready to have me.

Epilogue

I Think of You

I think of you often.

And I think whenever you think of a person often, you should let them know that.

Because no one ever says it enough, even though it's so true. And I think if they knew you thought of them that often and smiled, it would make them smile too. I think a person should know that there isn't a day that goes by that you don't think of them. And I think you should let them know that they mean the world to you.

I think I should let you know that you are my brightest spot on some of my darkest days. And that I will always have a place in my heart for you. And that the thought of your smile makes me smile. And that I still know what you smell like, and I still miss it. That I wish my bed was warmed by you. Or that I could at least kiss your lips when you came home at night. How sometimes I wish we had the luxury of time and space and innocence so the nights didn't seem so short. And the wait didn't seem so long.

I think I should let you know that you've destroyed me. And I've fallen. Despite logic and best efforts and knowing better. Fallen. Too hard. Too fast. And even after putting myself back on my feet, my heartstrings remain tethered to yours. Tangled in an all-too-complicated web. It shouldn't have to be this hard.

I think I should tell you that I'm scared. And I'm broken-hearted. Because I know you'll never change. And we will never be an us. Not because you're old and stubborn and arrogant and don't want to. But because I know where you're at. I hear you, but disagree. And I know how crazy complicated it is. I understand these things you think I do not. More than you think I ever could. It's hard, yes, but not impossible.

Or I think I should just skip that part, and simply tell you that I love you. I wish it were easy. My heart will be waiting. I'll still be standing here. And I think of you often.

About the author

With a penchant for the written word since childhood, Jennifer has been published in various magazines, newspapers, and other publications since her teenage years. Growing up on the tiny island nation of St. Maarten in the Caribbean, she was one of the founding members and editor-in-chief of the island's formidable teen newspaper, Teen Times.

When writing hasn't consumed her every thought until 2:00 AM, she enjoys reading, listening to audiobooks, rock climbing and hitting the Florida beaches with her daughters Sophie and Mila. The trio also love spending time with their guinea pig, Fluffy and their red-husky, Kyro.

Jennifer writes about love, heartache, trauma and the tough life lessons that going and growing through breast cancer has taught her. She has compiled a selection of her poetry on love and heartache in her first book *Fairytales & Lies*.

fairytalesandliesbook@gmail.com